D1301804

Words Every Woman Should Remember

We wish to thank Susan Polis Schutz for permission to reprint the following poems that appear in this publication: "Be a woman who…," "Sometimes you think that you…," "Go beyond yourself…," "You have to find a way…," "Successful women have these…," "People will tell you…," "Find happiness in nature…," "Give yourself the freedom…," "If you ever find yourself…," and "The love of a family…." Copyright © 1982, 1983, 1984, 1986, 1988, 1992, 2001, 2004 by Stephen Schutz and Susan Polis Schutz. And for "This life is yours…" and "Many people go…." Copyright © 1979, 1980 by Continental Publications. All rights reserved.

Library of Congress Control Number: 2017959504
ISBN: 978-1-68088-217-9

▉ and Blue Mountain Press are registered in U.S. Patent and Trademark Office.
Certain trademarks are used under license.

Acknowledgments appear on page 92.

Printed in China.
First Printing: 2018

✪ This book is printed on recycled paper.

This book is printed on paper that has been specially produced to be acid free (neutral pH) and contains no groundwood or unbleached pulp. It conforms with the requirements of the American National Standards Institute, Inc., so as to ensure that this book will last and be enjoyed by future generations.

Blue Mountain Arts, Inc.
P.O. Box 4549, Boulder, Colorado 80306

Words Every Woman Should Remember

Messages of Support, Encouragement, and Gratitude for All You Are and All You Do

Edited by Patricia Wayant

Blue Mountain Press™
Boulder, Colorado

Words Every Woman Should Remember

Take a moment to think about
how many people have smiled
    because of you —
about all the lives you've changed
    for the better,
sometimes without even trying.

Take a moment to look back
at all the joy you've caused
and all the good you've done,
even when you thought you were
    at your worst.

Take a moment to remember
how much love you've sent out there
and how much you matter to people,
just because you're you.

— Irina Vasilescu

❁ *You are a bright, talented, compassionate, one-of-a-kind, absolutely fantastic human being!*

❁ *You bring cheer to so many people just by your presence in their lives.*

❁ *You inspire others with your kindness and compassion.*

❁ *You make every day count.*

❁ *You are loved and admired more than you'll ever know.*

You ou are a blessing to every life you touch.
You have made impressions on people
and have changed their lives.
You give of yourself without expectation
and give your love without conditions.
You take on the problems of others
as your own,
and you never complain or grow weary.
You are a very special person
who has touched so many lives
in so many amazing ways
that will never be forgotten.
You make this world a better place.

— *Marni Alward*

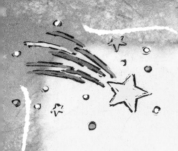

Don't you dare — even for an instant —
think that you don't deserve or "need"
the good things that come your way!
You deserve the very best,
and you shouldn't be afraid to ask for it
or accept it with open arms
when it's offered to you.
You work hard
and put in the time and effort
to get the job done.
You should receive the greatest rewards ever
in return for all your hard work.
You deserve the best in every way.

— Ashley Rice

✿ *Your presence adds something special and invaluable to the world. You bring joy to those who love you and a smile to everyone you meet.* (Star Nakamoto)

✿ *All the small things you do every day add up to something pretty significant.*

✿ *Compliments are someone's way of letting you know how special you are. Accept them freely.*

✿ *Over a lifetime, it's the moments you take to help a friend in need, push a child on a swing, or encourage someone else's dream that will be remembered.*

✿ *Pat yourself on the back and smile, because all your hard work and dedication haven't gone unnoticed.*
(Lamisha Serf-Walls)

✿ *Each dawn is the beginning of a new life. Live life day by day to understand the joy that is in your heart.* (Louise Bradford Lowell)

✿ *Give all you have without looking for something in return. Reach out for that which you can attain and not for that which is impossible. Be all you can, for only then will you awaken to the person you want to be.* (Joan Benicken)

✿ *As soon as you trust yourself, you will know how to live.* (Johann Wolfgang von Goethe)

✿ *No one will ever know you as well as you know yourself.*

Don't worry about the paths you should have taken or the opportunities you ignored. Instead, breathe in the life that surrounds you — let it fill your soul with light and hope.

Reflect on the past and all the memories, good and bad, that have made you who you are today.

Life can be so busy, and we sometimes take for granted the important little things that make us smile. Look at the sunset, share a cup of coffee with your best friend, or hear the wind rustle through the trees. Take some time to listen to life and feel the sun on your face. Stop to watch butterflies in your garden.

The gifts of beauty, inspiration, love, and reflection are all around you.

— Carol Schelling

✿ Don't run through life so fast that you forget not only where you've been but also where you're going. Life is not a race but a journey to be savored each step of the way. (Nancye Sims)

✿ When others are rushing around, take time to stop and appreciate the moment.

✿ Adopt the pace of nature: her secret is patience. (Ralph Waldo Emerson)

✿ If you are doing the best you can, then that's all you can do.

*A*t times, we can get so caught up in reaching our destination that we forget to appreciate our journey. Life is filled with problems to solve, lessons to learn, and, most of all, experiences to enjoy.

Focus on the journey, and never let a stumble in the road define who you are, where you are going, or how far you have come. It is important to slow down, enjoy life, and know that although the road you travel is yours alone, your present situation is not your final destination.

Sometimes the smallest step in the right direction ends up being the biggest leap of your life.

— Eileen Rosenfeld

This life is yours
Take the power
to choose what you want to do
and do it well
Take the power
to love what you want in life
and love it honestly
Take the power
to walk in the forest
and be a part of nature
Take the power
to control your own life
No one else can do it for you
Take the power
to make your life
healthy
exciting
worthwhile
and very happy

— Susan Polis Schutz

❁ *To put the world in order, we must first put the nation in order; to put the nation in order, we must first put the family in order; to put the family in order, we must first cultivate our personal life; and to cultivate our personal life, we must first set our hearts right. (Confucius)*

❁ *Allow plenty of room for what matters most in your life — love, friendship, family, and laughter.*

❁ *Believe you can make great things happen, and chances are they will.*

❁ *The only one responsible for your life is you.*

❁ *Every day has the potential to be amazing.*

Remember All That
It Means to Be a Woman

A woman is a person of strength. Yet it is in her weakest moments that she is strongest.

A woman is a person of intuition. She can "fine tune" her inner voice and find that place of wisdom within her soul.

A woman is a person of independence. She stands proudly on her own, knowing she can always count on herself.

A woman is a person of trust. Confide in her and she'll lock it in her heart forever. Betray her trust and you've lost a true friend.

A woman is a person of vulnerability. She sees the world with a kaleidoscope of passion, inviting others to see beyond the black and white.

A woman is a person of emotion. She pours it in different quantities but never runs out.

A woman is a person of gratitude. She never takes for granted the beauty of human generosity.

A woman is a person of wisdom and maturity. Through her maturity, she gains wisdom — and with that wisdom, she matures.

A woman is a person of awareness and spirit. She flows with the universe... to be where she is meant to be.

— Debbie Burton-Peddle

❀ Don't be afraid to show the world your true, authentic self.

❀ Be honest with yourself, as well as with others.

❀ You don't always have to follow the crowd. You can make your own way and let the crowd follow you.

❀ You deserve complete and total respect.

❀ Don't ever downplay your abilities or your special charm. Keep living your life the best way you know how — with persistence, patience, and determination. *(Vickie M. Worsham)*

Be true to your dreams, and keep them alive. Never let anyone change your mind about what you feel you can achieve.

Be true to the light that is deep within you. Hold on to your faith, hope, and joy for life. Keep good thoughts in your mind and good feelings in your heart.

Be true to yourself in the paths that you choose. Follow your talents and passions; don't take the roads others say you must follow because they are the most popular.

Most of all, never forget that there is no brighter light than the one within you, and follow your inner light to your own personal greatness.

— *Jacqueline Schiff*

Refuse negative thoughts;
replace them with positive ones.
Look for the good things in your life
and make a point of appreciating them.
Believe in yourself and know that you
    have the power.
You are ultimately the one in charge
    of your life
and the only person in the world who
    can change it.
No matter how much others are
    pulling for you
or how much anyone else cares,
you must do what needs to be done
to make your present and future
everything you want and need it to be.

— Barbara Cage

✿ *You are in control of your own thoughts.*

✿ *The happiest people are those who look out on the world with a positive mindset. They focus on what they have, instead of what they don't have, and find joy in life's simplest pleasures.*

✿ *Fretting over the past will get you nowhere fast.*

✿ *Within the scope of the universe, it's likely that the very thing causing you the most stress is actually insignificant.*

✿ *Embrace what is good in your life, and let go of the rest.*

*O*ur deepest fear is not that we are inadequate. Our deepest fear is that we are powerful beyond measure. It is our light, not our darkness, that most frightens us. We ask ourselves, Who am I to be brilliant, gorgeous, talented, fabulous? Actually, who are you not to be? You are a child of God. Your playing small does not serve the world. There is nothing enlightened about shrinking so that other people won't feel insecure around you. We are all meant to shine, as children do. We were born to make manifest the glory of God that is within us. It's not just in some of us; it's in everyone. And as we let our own light shine, we unconsciously give other people permission to do the same. As we are liberated from our own fear, our presence automatically liberates others.

— Marianne Williamson

✿ *Sometimes it is out of our greatest fears that come our most beneficial experiences.*

✿ *Don't let your fears prevent you from pursuing your dreams.*

✿ *You must do the thing you think you cannot do.* (Eleanor Roosevelt)

✿ *Fear less, hope more; eat less, chew more; whine less, breathe more; talk less, say more; hate less, love more; and all good things are yours.* (Swedish Proverb)

✿ *Worry never solves anything.*

✿ Determine your own worth by yourself, and do not be dependent on another's judgment of you. *(Debbi Oehman)*

✿ Look into your heart, search your dreams, and be honest about what you really want; then do whatever it takes to get it. Live like you mean it. Believe you can... and you will! *(Barbara Cage)*

✿ Do something totally out of character once in a while — you might discover something new about yourself.

✿ It matters what you think. Speak up. Voice your opinions. Share your ideas.

✿ Life is an adventure, dare it. *(Mother Teresa)*

Sometimes it's your turn
to play the music
to sing the song
to make a joyful noise
that can be heard
loud and clear

sometimes it's your time
to take a stance
or a stand
or maybe to just jump up
and be the first
to dance

and sometimes it is your moment
to step up and step out
of your comfort zone
and claim your place
at the top
or in the circle or wherever
life is beckoning you
to show up

— Minx Boren

*B*e a woman who
knows what she wants to do
and does it
A woman who
is not afraid to
speak out for what she believes
A woman who
is kind and good and giving
A woman who
sets high goals for herself
and achieves them
A woman who
is beautiful on the outside
and the inside
A woman who
understands herself and
is in complete charge of her life
A woman who
is intelligent and sensitive
strong and able
A woman who
gives so much to her friends
to her family
to everyone
— Susan Polis Schutz

❁ *Trust your gut, pay attention to what your mind is telling you, and always follow your heart.*

❁ *Sometimes the hardest times in our lives are what push us further, inspire us to be bolder, teach us about real hope, and help us to become the greatest version of that person we always hoped we'd be.* (Ashley Rice)

❁ *For all the days when nothing seems to be going right... remember there will be plenty of days when everything goes better than expected.*

❁ *It's important to believe in yourself and when you feel like you have the right idea, to stay with it.* (Rosa Parks)

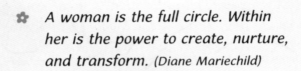

✿ *A woman is the full circle. Within her is the power to create, nurture, and transform.* (Diane Mariechild)

✿ *Recognize and appreciate your own talents.*

✿ *It's not what you do but who you are that counts.*

✿ *By being yourself, you help others to be themselves.*

✿ *Be someone others look up to.*

*B*e someone others admire
for the life that you lead and
the kindness that is such a
sweet and natural part of you...

for the way you treat other people...

for how easily a smile finds its way
to your face...

for the work that you do and the
places your journeys take you...

for your dedication to all the right
things and your devotion to
your family...

for how completely you care and
how willingly you are always there
for the people who need you...

for being the light that you are...
in the lives of others.
— L. N. Mallory

*Sometimes you
think that you
need to be perfect
that you cannot
make mistakes
At these times
you put so much
pressure on yourself
Try to realize
that you are
a human being
like everyone else —
capable of
reaching great potential
but not capable of
being perfect
Just do your best
and realize that
this is enough*

— *Susan Polis Schutz*

❀ *Perfectionism is not a quest for the best. It is a pursuit of the worst in ourselves, the part that tells us that nothing we do will ever be good enough — that we should try again. (Julia Cameron)*

❀ *Superwoman is a fictional character; she does not actually exist.*

❀ *Preserving your sanity is more important than meeting a deadline.*

❀ *You are limited by the number of things you can do at once.*

❀ *You can — and will — check off every item on your to-do list in time.*

You can cry, you know.

You can let it all out.
You can let your hot tears fall
silently on your pillow
or you can let each drop
pound down with force,
screaming out all those things
you've kept inside.

It might make you feel better
or it might make you feel worse,
but it will make you feel.

It will stop this machine
from chugging along.
Always working.
Always moving.
Never happy,
never satisfied.

You can feel this pain.
You're allowed to be hurt.
Feeling does not make
you weak.

These tears are not you.
These mountains you can't get over
are not you.
These mistakes
and circumstances
are not you.

You are bright
and beautiful
and full of hope.
You are strong
and brave
and a little bit tired.

So let go, dear one.
Let go of the perception of perfection.
Because you know that you are not
and it's okay if they see it too.

— Jenna Brown

❀ *Every woman needs a place she can call her own — whether it's a whole room, a spot in the garden, or a special chair — where she can relax and be herself.*

❀ *You're not being selfish when you do something nice for yourself.*

❀ *Take a little time every day just for yourself — even if it's only fifteen minutes.*

❀ *Slow down, embrace solitude, and discover your inner joy.*

Let go...
of guilt; it's okay to make
the same mistakes again.

Let go...
of obsessions; they seldom
turn out the way you planned.

Let go...
of hate; it's a waste of love.

Let go...
of blaming others; you are
responsible for your own destiny.

Let go...
of fear; it's a waste of faith.

Let go...
of despair; change comes from
acceptance and forgiveness.

Let go...
of the past; the future is
here — right now.

— Kathleen O'Brien

✿ *Nothing can bring you peace but yourself.* (Ralph Waldo Emerson)

✿ *When you accept what is — without any judgment — you will find serenity.*

✿ *The peace you are looking for is inside yourself.*

✿ *Schedule time in your day when you can let your body and mind be at total rest.*

✿ *Fill your heart with the kindness of friends, the caring of everyone you love, and the richness of memories you wouldn't trade for anything.* (Douglas Pagels)

Here's the thing... life changes a lot.
So cherish the things you love most,
and keep a sharp eye out
for the good in everyday life.
Be aware of pitfalls —
those situations that don't feel quite right —
and keep peace in your heart.

Even when it's raining,
when the world around you
is spinning and flailing,
when the door won't open
and the car won't start —
keep peace in your heart.

— Ashley Rice

Good or bad, feelings need expression; they must be recognized and given freedom to reveal themselves. Put away the myth that says you must be strong enough to face the whole world with a smile and a brave attitude all of the time. You have your feelings that say otherwise, so admit that they are there. Use their healing power to put the past behind you, and realize those expressive stirrings in your heart are very much a part of you. Use them to get better, to find peace within, to be true to yourself.

— Barbara J. Hall

✿ *Don't be afraid to feel what you're feeling. Try to remember that you are not alone. Remember that you are very loved, very needed, and very special.* (T. L. DiMonte)

✿ *The greater part of our happiness or misery depends on our dispositions and not on our circumstances.* (Martha Washington)

✿ *One can be the master of what one does, but never of what one feels.* (Gustave Flaubert)

✿ *Follow your feelings and consider them to be the voice of your innermost beliefs.* (George Sand)

✿ A caring word or a smile given freely has the power to turn someone's life around.

✿ Go beyond yourself and reach out to other people with a sincere love, respect, caring, and understanding of their needs. (Susan Polis Schutz)

✿ One act of kindness can lead to another and then another. It all begins with one person.

✿ By opening your heart to the people you meet, you invite them to open their hearts to you.

✿ Make it a priority to be loving, compassionate, and kind.

In our busy lives, we let life carry us away on a never-ending road filled with the responsibilities of a day-to-day existence.

We often forget that there is more along the way than just bills to pay, phone calls to return, and errands to run. There are people in our lives who need to be hugged, who need to be loved. There are people in our lives who need their accomplishments noticed and praised. We need to remember how fragile hearts can be, how quickly a soul can grow weary, how fast a spirit can break.

We forget that a heart is like a garden that needs to be tended to and nourished with what only another heart can give — love and appreciation, devotion and honesty.

— Tracia Gloudemans

✿ *The strength of a woman is found in her ability to manage multiple crises while also maintaining her composure.*

✿ *The best protection any woman can have... is courage. (Elizabeth Cady Stanton)*

✿ *We must have perseverance and above all confidence in ourselves. We must believe that we are gifted for something and that this thing must be attained. (Marie Curie)*

✿ *When you get into a tight place and everything goes against you until it seems that you cannot hold on for a minute longer, never give up then, for that is just the place and time when the tide will turn. (Harriet Beecher Stowe)*

*D*raw strength from the good things in your life — from the simplest to the greatest. Whether it's a pretty little flower, a kind word from a friend, a walk in your favorite place, or a beautiful sunset — draw strength from anything good that touches your heart or your day.

Draw strength from those who love you — those who make your life richer by being a part of your days; those who will be there for you not only on sunny days but also on the cloudy ones, and who will hold you in the storms of life.

Have faith in yourself. Draw strength from your faith. And know in your heart that you have the strength to make it through anything.

— Nancye Sims

✿ *Nobody's life is without challenges and hardships, bad days and even worse days, but everybody gets a shot at new days and second chances.*

✿ *You're going to make some mistakes — don't dwell on them.*

✿ *There are some things you cannot change — accept that and move on.*

✿ *Don't let setbacks and disappointments discourage you — you have untapped reserves of inner strength.*

✿ *Let any regrets you may have be a springboard for your future.*

Believe

you are beautiful;
cherish your
uniqueness
and be who you are;
through every hardship,
trust yourself
to overcome.
Be strong
when you can,
cry when you can't;
be wise of the past
and embrace now!
Reach out
when you are safe,
hide when you are not,
laugh often...
and listen carefully.
And never be afraid
to love yourself,
for that is where
all peace... is born.

— Pam Reinke

Strong women are those who know the road ahead will be strewn with obstacles, but they still choose to walk it because it's the right one for them.

Strong women are those who make mistakes, who admit to them, learn from those failures, and then use that knowledge.

Strong women are easily hurt, but they still extend their hearts and hands, knowing the risk and accepting the pain when it comes.

Strong women are sometimes beat down by life, but they still stand back up and step forward again.

Strong women are afraid. They face fear and move ahead to the future, as uncertain as it can be.

Strong women are not those who succeed the first time. They're the ones who fail time and again, but still keep trying until they succeed.

Strong women face the daily trials of life, sometimes with a tear, but always with their heads held high as the new day dawns.

— *Brenda Hager*

There are two very easy things
to do in life:
One is to blame someone else
for anything and everything,
the other is to make excuses to yourself.
That's just the way life is.
Either way, you deny yourself
of truly being responsible
for your own life and your own happiness.
Quit making excuses.
Be the person you really want to be,
and know that the fewer excuses you make,
the better you will feel about
all the rewards that come your way.

— Deanna Beisser

✿ *Whatever you are trying to avoid won't go away until you confront it.* (Author Unknown)

✿ *Spend less time agonizing over decisions and more time acting on what you think needs to be done.*

✿ *Be receptive to views and opinions that are different from your own.*

✿ *Advice is one of the easiest things to give and the hardest things to receive.*

✿ *No one can make you feel inferior without your consent.* (Eleanor Roosevelt)

❀ You have to find a way to balance your work, private life, and everything else that is important to you. *(Susan Polis Schutz)*

❀ Don't get stuck repeating the same mistakes — whether it's your lifestyle, your diet, or your relationships.

❀ You always have choices, and by not expressing your opinion, you are making a choice.

❀ Don't commit yourself to a project just because it's what others want you to do. Be sure it's something you want too.

❀ When your heart is in the right place, you can never go wrong.

Always remember, no matter what is going on in your life, it is your responsibility to choose how you respond. This does not mean you will not hurt. This does not translate to you should ignore what you feel. Not being a victim and taking responsibility means: feel the pain, honor the shock, look for the lesson, and keep on moving in a way that honors who you really are. You are Spirit in a body having a temporary human experience. Your experiences may knock you down, but it is your responsibility not to let them keep you down.

— *Iyanla Vanzant*

In times of doubt, remember...
When you toss
even the tiniest of pebbles
into the ocean,
ripples do form.
Small, radiating circles
that bring waves of change
to the flowing current of the water.
Within the ocean of humanity,
you are the pebble.
You have the ability to create the waves
and bring change to every life
you touch.

— J. Marie Larson

✿ Every big change starts with a small step.

✿ If you don't like how things are going, do something about it!

✿ Be open to new ideas, new people, and new adventures.

✿ Don't settle for "good enough." Keep learning, growing, and changing.

✿ Everything in life that we really accept undergoes a change. *(Katherine Mansfield)*

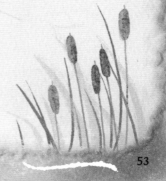

Successful women have these
twelve qualities in common
They have confidence in themselves
They have a very strong sense of purpose
They never have excuses for not doing something
They always try their hardest for perfection
They never consider the idea of failing
They work extremely hard toward their goals
They know who they are
They understand their weaknesses
as well as their strong points
They can accept and benefit from criticism
They know when to defend what they are doing
They are creative
They are not afraid to be a little different
in finding innovative solutions
that will enable them to achieve their dreams

— Susan Polis Schutz

✿ *Success is often a personal achievement that goes beyond material wealth and reputation. It can be something as rewarding as making a nourishing meal for your family or growing a flower garden from seed.*

✿ *To guarantee success, act as if it were impossible to fail.* (Dorothea Brande)

✿ *Energy and persistence conquer all things.* (Benjamin Franklin)

✿ *The most important thing in our lives is what we are doing now.* (Author Unknown)

✿ *There is no such thing as failure — only lessons learned.*

There are women who make things
better... simply by showing up. There
are women who make things happen.
There are women who make their
way. There are women who make a
difference. There are women who
make us smile. There are women who
do not make excuses and women who
cannot be replaced. There are women
of wit and wisdom who — through
strength and courage — make it
through. There are women who
change the world every day... women
like you.

— Ashley Rice

✿ *Follow your passion; appreciate your own self-worth.*

✿ *Always have something to hope for.*

✿ *Purpose is knowing what you want to do and where you want to go in life. Passion is letting nothing stand in the way of getting there.* (Vickie M. Worsham)

✿ *People will tell you that you are wrong. It has not and cannot be done! Some will even say you are crazy. But if you feel it is right, pursue your idea, your dream, your creativity. That is what makes new discoveries, beauty, and truth.* (Susan Polis Schutz)

✿ *Have something unique in your life that's just for you — whether it's a special interest, a particular hobby, or a favorite tradition.*

✿ *When the road curves to lead you into new discoveries... let it take you. When the wind pulls under your wings and urges you on to greater heights... let it take you.* (Susan A. J. Lyttek)

✿ *Remember how it was to be a child. Take your shoes off! Explore! Play a game! Let your imagination transport you to wherever you want to go!*

✿ *It's okay to color outside the lines.*

✿ *Be happy now!*

The Habits Manifesto

What we do every day matters more than what we do once in a while.

Make it easy to do right and hard to go wrong.

Focus on actions, not outcomes.

By giving something up, we may gain.

Things often get harder before they get easier.

When we give more to ourselves, we can ask more from ourselves.

We're not very different from other people, but those differences are very important.

It's easier to change our surroundings than ourselves.

We can't make people change, but when we change, others may change.

We should make sure the things we do to feel better don't make us feel worse.

We manage what we monitor.

Once we're ready to begin, begin now.

— *Gretchen Rubin*

✿ Now and then it's good to pause in our pursuit of happiness and just be happy. *(Guillaume Apollinaire)*

✿ Don't let anyone hold your happiness in their hands; hold it in yours, so it will always be within your reach. *(Nancye Sims)*

✿ Real happiness comes from knowing who you are and being the best that you can be.

✿ Keep knocking, and the joy inside will eventually open a window and look out to see who's there. *(Rumi)*

ind happiness in nature
in the beauty of a mountain
in the serenity of the sea
Find happiness in friendship
in the fun of doing things together
in the sharing and understanding
Find happiness in your family
in the stability of knowing
that someone cares
in the strength of love and honesty
Find happiness in yourself
in your mind and body
in your values and achievements
Find happiness in
everything
you
do

— Susan Polis Schutz

❀ Each new day is a blank page in the diary of your life. Every day you're given a chance to determine what the words will say and how the story will unfold. *(Douglas Pagels)*

❀ Give yourself the freedom to try out new things. Don't be so set in your ways that you can't grow. *(Susan Polis Schutz)*

❀ The difference between ordinary and extraordinary is that little extra. *(Author Unknown)*

❀ Every now and then, go ahead and do something wild and outrageous!

❀ Dance like nobody's watching; love like you've never been hurt. Sing like nobody's listening; live like it's heaven on earth. *(Author Unknown)*

*D*on't just have minutes in the day, have moments in time. Balance out any bad with the good you can provide. Know that you are capable of amazing results. Surprise yourself by discovering new strength inside.

Do things no one else would even dream of. There is no greater gift than the kind of inner beauty you possess. Do the things you do... with love.

Walk along the pathways that enrich your happiness. Taking care of the "little things" is a big necessity. Don't be afraid of testing your courage. Life is short, but it's long enough to have excitement and serenity.

Don't let the important things go unsaid. Do the things that brighten your life and help you on your way.

— *Collin McCarty*

❁ Take time each day to think about the blessings in your life.

❁ Find at least one thing every day to be grateful for.

❁ Every day, be full of awareness of the beauty around you. Be full of gratitude for friends and family, for the goodness you find in others, for your health and all you're capable of. (Barbara Cage)

❁ Joy is not in things; it is in us. (Richard Wagner)

❁ Appreciation is a wonderful thing; it makes what is excellent in others belong to us as well. (Voltaire)

*G*ratitude unlocks the fullness of life. Gratitude makes things right. It turns what we have into enough, and more. It turns denial into acceptance, chaos to order, confusion to clarity. It can turn a meal into a feast, a house into a home, a stranger into a friend. It turns problems into gifts, failures into successes, the unexpected into perfect timing, and mistakes into important events. It can turn an existence into a real life, and disconnected situations into important and beneficial lessons. Gratitude makes sense of our past, brings peace for today, and creates a vision for tomorrow.

— *Melody Beattie*

So often, it's the little things in life
that make the biggest difference...
Sometimes a word offered
at the perfect moment
can bring someone comfort.
A hug wrapped in loving arms
sends a caring message to the heart,
and one smile can chase the blues away
and make you smile again too.

A little time shared with someone
who cares about you
can sprinkle sunshine into lonely moments
by letting someone know how much
they mean to you.

Life offers many opportunities
to give away a little of ourselves
    each day —
to share the joy of life
and living in this world together,
to widen that circle of friendship
wherever we go.

If we could all make a point
of remembering those little things,
we could all make a difference every day.

A well-placed word, a tender touch,
a heartfelt hug, a sincere smile...
are ways to spread sunshine
all along life's path.
                        — Barbara J. Hall

✿ *Notice serendipitous moments and events happening in your life. They may be trying to tell you something.*

✿ *Accept help from others when it's offered; offer help to others when you can.*

✿ *Spend more time with the positive people in your life and less time with the negative ones.*

✿ *If you have much, give your wealth; if you have little, give your heart.* (Author Unknown)

✿ *Sometimes it is simply best just to wait and see what happens.* (George Sand)

Stretching herself too thin, a woman breaks her connections.

Staying too busy, she has no time.

Doing for others, she neglects herself.

Defining herself only through others, she loses her own definition.

The wise woman waters her own garden first.

— *Nu Shu Proverb*

*I*t's so easy for women to slip into
    self-doubt and feeling inadequate.
After all,
we shoulder a lot of responsibilities —
    being supportive of our mates,
    nurturing our children,
    staying in touch with extended family,
    holding down jobs
    while holding down the fort at home.

No wonder we sometimes feel
    anxious, exhausted, and insecure.

We need to know
    we're not alone.
We need to hear
    that other women share our experiences.
We need reassurance
    that there's someone who understands —
    someone who's been there, done that.

As women, we take turns encouraging,
    supporting, and cheering one another on.

— BJ Gallagher

✿ *Always have at least one true friend you can talk with about anything.*

✿ *We don't make it alone in this world. We're lucky that there are people placed in our path to guide us, protect us, and touch our lives. (Julia Escobar)*

✿ *Friendship is the inexpressible comfort of feeling safe with a person, having neither to weigh thoughts or measure words. (George Eliot)*

✿ *Learn from the women who came before you.*

✿ *Many people will walk in and out of your life, but only true friends will leave footprints in your heart. (Eleanor Roosevelt)*

✿ *Surround yourself with people who will support and encourage you and who make you feel good.*

✿ *Be a good listener — sometimes all the person you're listening to really wants is to be heard.*

✿ *We all need a person to understand — someone to share our thoughts with and always be around in time of need.* (Louise Bradford Lowell)

✿ *Look for the good in others — everybody has his or her own song to sing. Give people a chance to love you, for that is how you learn to love.* (Melissa Ososki)

Many people
go from one thing
to another
searching for happiness
but with each new venture
they find themselves
more confused
and less happy
until they discover
that what they are
searching for
is inside themselves
and what will make them happy
is sharing their real selves
with the one they love

— Susan Polis Schutz

If you ever find yourself chasing after the wrong things, remember this — the love between a family, and the moments spent together with your family and friends, are the only answer to all that is crazy in the world.

— Susan Polis Schutz

Accomplishing your daily goals has a place, but the heart has a valid agenda of its own. When you can look back on a day and find within it even one warm memory of a single touching story, you've paid attention to your heart. That's worth whatever time it took.

— Victoria Moran

❁ *Having someplace to go is home. Having someone to love is family. Having both is a blessing.* (Author Unknown)

❁ *Cherish the times spent with family and loved ones. Those are the greatest memories you will ever make.*

❁ *A woman's heart grows in proportion to the size of her family.*

❁ *The love of a family toward one another can mold one's attitude forever toward the world.* (Susan Polis Schutz)

❁ You will find as you look back upon your life that the moments that stand out, the moments when you have really lived, are the moments when you have done things in a spirit of love. *(Henry Drummond)*

❁ Look for love all around you... in the eyes of a child, the touch of a pet, or the face of a stranger.

❁ You can never say "I love you" too many times to the people you care about.

❁ Sometimes a hug is the best medicine.

❁ The love we give away is the only love we keep. *(Elbert Hubbard)*

We don't create a healthy relationship by simply finding the "right person." We create the possibility for this kind of intimate dance by first being the right person and doing our own purposeful work — both internally and in the world — so we can understand ourselves and fully become who we are. By first listening deeply to our inner voice, giving space for our own truth to emerge, and then acting from that awareness, we open ourselves to love. From that inner spaciousness, we can skillfully and lovingly offer that same attentive listening to another, with both honest curiosity and gracious appreciation. Only then are we able to allow ourselves to discover the essence and soul of another human being.

— Minx Boren

❀ *You may not realize it, but you have a lot of wisdom and experience to share.*

❀ *Be a mentor to somebody.*

❀ *There are people who look up to you and depend on you.*

❀ *What goes around comes around.*

❀ *The praise and good feelings you give to others will come back to you.*

The priceless gifts we give each other
are not the ones wrapped
in fancy paper,
but the gifts we give when
we give of ourselves.
It is the love that we share.
It is the comfort we lend at times of need.
It is the moments we spend together
helping each other follow our dreams.
The most priceless gifts we can give
are the understanding and caring
that come from the heart.
And each and every one of us
has these gifts to offer...
through the gift of ourselves.

— Ben Daniels

*T*rue beauty is not related to what color your hair is or what color your eyes are. True beauty is about who you are as a human being, your principles, your moral compass.

— Ellen DeGeneres

*P*eople are like stained glass windows; they sparkle and shine when the sun is out, but when the darkness sets in, their true beauty is revealed only if there is a light from within.

— Author Unknown

✿   *You are beautiful when you smile.*

✿   *You are beautiful when you laugh.*

✿   *You are beautiful when you stand up for what you believe.*

✿   *You are beautiful with or without makeup.*

✿   *You are beautiful when you are proud of your body — imperfections and all!*

✿   *You are beautiful when you speak and act from the heart.*

We all become different people
as we grow older,
with different hopes and dreams,
goals and achievements,
memories and feelings.
No one can ever say that, as a person,
they are all they can be,
for it is then that they
have stopped growing from within.
We must continue to grow,
to dream,
to make new memories,
and to do whatever gives us peace
within ourselves.

— *Shirley Vander Pol*

❂ Feel good about your age, knowing it has nothing to do with who you are and everything to do with what you mean to others. *(Debbie Burton-Peddle)*

❂ Every day is a gift; every moment is an opportunity to unwrap that gift.

❂ Gray hair is earned — it's a reminder of all you've accomplished.

❂ It is never too late to be what you might have been. *(George Eliot)*

❂ Don't ever stop loving; don't ever stop believing; don't ever stop dreaming your dreams. *(Laine Parsons)*

People like you make the world
   a better place,
because you think of ways
to make a positive difference
   in the lives of others.

People like you make
those you come in contact with
   feel special
by acts of kindness and deeds
   of thoughtfulness.

People like you deserve the best out of life,
because that's what you give.
May your kindness and good deeds
always come back to you.
                              — Barbara Cage

❁ You have a remarkable ability to lift
    people's spirits, find the good in every
    situation, and set a wonderful example
    of patience and understanding. (Perri
    Elizabeth Hogan)

❁ There is no one else on the planet like
    you, and there never will be.

❁ You make a positive difference in the
    lives of countless people.

❁ You deserve everything good that
    comes your way.

❁ For all the times it's gone unsaid...
    "Thank you!"

✿ *You're smart.*

✿ *You're creative.*

✿ *You're thoughtful.*

✿ *You're kind.*

✿ *You're charismatic.*

✿ *You're nurturing.*

✿ *You're adventurous.*

✿ *You're full of possibilities.*

✿ *You're perfect just the way you are.*

Look in the mirror and
see what others see —
a talented, uplifting,
and magnificent woman
who can do anything
and everything she wants.

Believe in your heart
that you have the power
to grab hold of your future
and mold it into the things
you have always dreamed of.

Trust in your soul
that you are capable of doing
all that needs to be done.

Know that you are
incredible in every way
and see yourself
as others see you...
as an intelligent
and spectacular woman.

— Lamisha Serf-Walls

There is no one in the past, present, or future who will ever offer the world what you do. No one will think, act, or smile exactly like you. No one will be able to come up with your unique points of view.

Don't hold back who you really are. When you are true to yourself, you glow. When you are passionate about your dreams, you shine. When you live fully, people are drawn to you. And then you can't help but make friends with good people: the ones who love you for just being you.

— *April Aragam*

✿ *You inspire so much joy in the lives of everyone who is lucky enough to know you.*
(Sydney Nelson)

✿ *The world relies on women like you.*

✿ *You are somebody's hero.*

✿ *You mean so much to so many, and though you may not realize it, there are a lot of people out there who love you and think about you and wish you life's best every day.*
(Linda E. Knight)

ou're a one-of-a-kind treasure, uniquely here in this space and time. You are here to shine in your own wonderful way, sharing your smile in the best way you can, and remembering all the while that a little light somewhere makes a brighter light everywhere. You can — and you do — make a wonderful contribution to this world.

You have qualities within you that many people would love to have, and those who really and truly know you... are so glad that they do. You have a big heart and a good and sensitive soul. You are gifted with thoughts and ways of seeing things that only special people know.

You know that life doesn't always play by the rules but that in the long run, everything will work out.

You understand that you and your actions are capable of turning anything around — and that joys once lost can always be found. There is a resolve and an inner reserve of strength in you that few ever get to see. You have so many treasures within — those you're only beginning to discover, and all the ones you're already aware of.

Never forget what a treasure you are. That special person in the mirror may not always get to hear all the compliments you so sweetly deserve, but you are so worthy of such an abundance... of friendship, joy, and love.

— *Douglas Pagels*

ACKNOWLEDGMENTS

We gratefully acknowledge the permission granted by the following authors, publishers, and authors' representatives to reprint poems or excerpts from their publications:

Eileen Rosenfeld for "At times, we can get so caught up...." Copyright © 2018 by Eileen Rosenfeld. All rights reserved.

Debbie Burton-Peddle for "Remember All That It Means to Be a Woman." Copyright © 2018 by Debbie Burton-Peddle. All rights reserved.

HarperCollins Publishers for "Our deepest fear is not..." from A RETURN TO LOVE: REFLECTIONS IN THE PRINCIPLES OF A COURSE IN MIRACLES by Marianne Williamson. Copyright © 1992 by Marianne Williamson. All rights reserved. And for "Accomplishing your daily..." from CREATING A CHARMED LIFE: SENSIBLE, SPIRITUAL SECRETS EVERY BUSY WOMAN SHOULD KNOW by Victoria Moran. Copyright © 1999 by Victoria Moran. All rights reserved.

Minx Boren for "Sometimes it's your turn..." from IT'S ALWAYS POSSIBLE and "We don't create a healthy..." from LOVE IS A JOURNEY. Copyright © 2014, 2015 by Minx Boren, MCC. All rights reserved.

Jeremy P. Tarcher/Putnam, an imprint of Penguin Publishing Group, a division of Penguin Random House LLC, for "Perfectionism is not a quest..." from THE ARTIST'S WAY: A SPIRITUAL PATH TO HIGHER CREATIVITY by Julia Cameron. Copyright © 1992 by Julia Cameron. All rights reserved.

Jenna Brown for "You can cry, you know" from "You Can Cry, You Know," *Thought Catalog* (blog), March 15, 2017, https://thoughtcatalog.com/jenna-brown/2017/03/you-can-cry-you-know/. Copyright © 2017 by Jenna Brown. All rights reserved.

Barbara J. Hall for "Good or bad, feelings need..." and "So often, it's the little things...." Copyright © 2018 by Barbara J. Hall. All rights reserved.

Pam Reinke for "Believe you are beautiful...." Copyright © 2006 by Pam Reinke. All rights reserved.

Deanna Beisser for "There are two very easy things...." Copyright © 2018 by Deanna Beisser. All rights reserved.

Fireside, a division of Simon & Schuster Adult Publishing Group, for "Always remember, no matter what..." from FAITH IN THE VALLEY: LESSONS FOR WOMEN ON THE JOURNEY TOWARD PEACE by Iyanla Vanzant. Copyright © 1996 by Iyanla Vanzant. All rights reserved.

J. Marie Larson for "In times of doubt...." Copyright © 2018 by J. Marie Larson. All rights reserved.

Vickie M. Worsham for "Purpose is knowing...." Copyright © 2018 by Vickie M. Worsham. All rights reserved.

Broadway Books, an imprint of the Crown Publishing Group, a division of Penguin Random House LLC, for "The Habits Manifesto" from BETTER THAN BEFORE by Gretchen Rubin. Copyright © 2015 by Gretchen Rubin. All rights reserved.